Love Songs

for Keyboard

Music arranged and processed by Barnes Music Engraving Ltd.,
East Sussex TN22 4HA, UK.

Compiled by Sadie Cook

Published 1994

215-2-1116

CARELESS WHISPER

Words & Music by George Michael and Andrew Ridgeley

Suggested Registration: Tenor Sax
Rhythm: 16 Beat
Tempo: ♩ = 74

I feel__ so un - sure as I take your hand, and lead you

to the dance floor. As the mu - sic dies, some - thing in your eyes___

calls to mind a sil - ver screen, and you're its sad good - bye. I'm ne - ver gon - na dance a - gain,

Close To You
(They Long To Be)

Words by Hal David / Music by Burt Bacharach

Suggested Registration: Vibraphone
Rhythm: Swing
Tempo: ♩ = 88

CRAZY FOR YOU

Words & Music by Jon Lind and John Bettis

Suggested Registration: Piano
Rhythm: Rock / Pop
Tempo: ♩ = 108

7

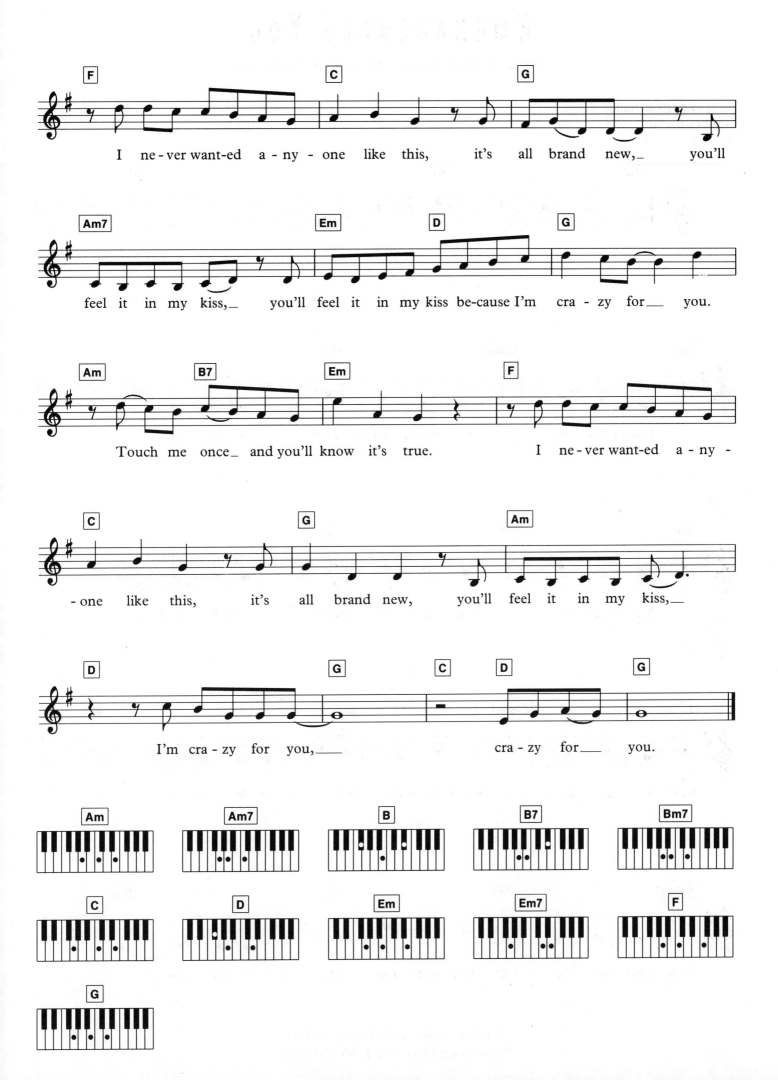

Embraceable You

Music and Lyrics by George Gershwin and Ira Gershwin

Suggested Registration: Piano
Rhythm: Swing
Tempo: ♩ = 104

Em - brace me my sweet, em - brace - a - ble you.____

Em - brace me you ir - re - place - a - ble you.____

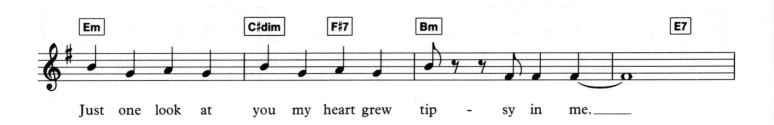

Just one look at you my heart grew tip - sy in me.____

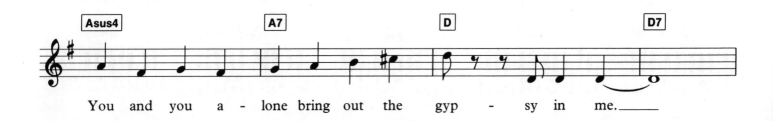

You and you a - lone bring out the gyp - sy in me.____

I love all the ma - ny charms a - bout you.___

A - bove all I want my arms a - bout you.___

Don't be a naugh - ty ba - by, come to Pa-pa, come to Pa-pa do.

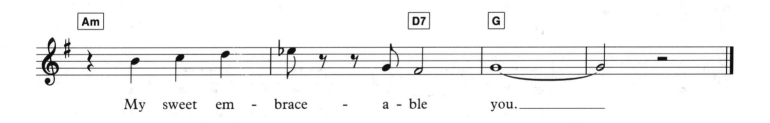

My sweet em - brace - a - ble you.___

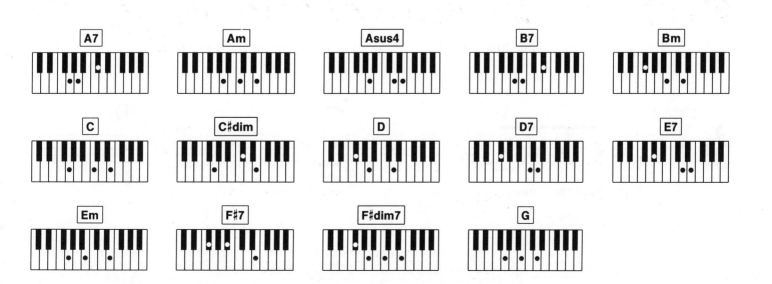

The First Time Ever I Saw Your Face

Words & Music by Ewan MacColl

Suggested Registration: Piano
Rhythm: Rock Ballad
Tempo: ♩ = 88

The first time ____ ev - er I saw your face, _____

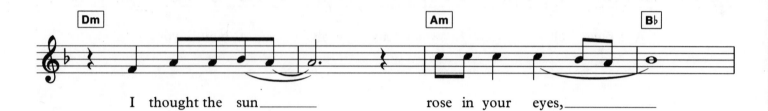

I thought the sun _____ rose in your eyes, _____

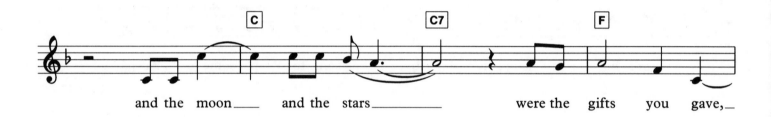

and the moon ____ and the stars _____ were the gifts you gave, __

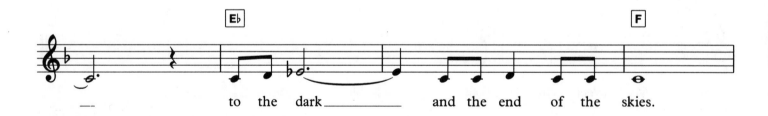

__ to the dark _____ and the end of the skies.

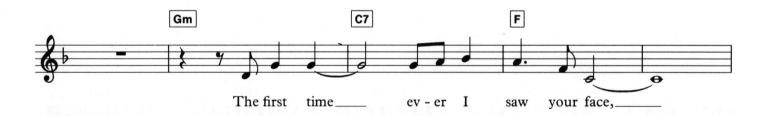

The first time ____ ev - er I saw your face, _____

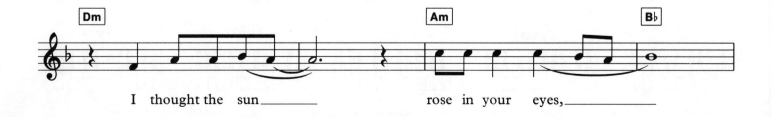

I thought the sun _____ rose in your eyes, _____

and the moon___ and the stars_____ were the gifts you gave,___

and last___ till the end___ of time my love.

The first time___ ev-er I saw your face,_____ your face,

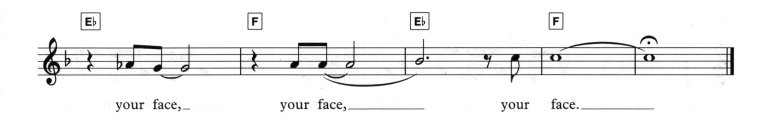

your face,_ your face,_____ your face._____

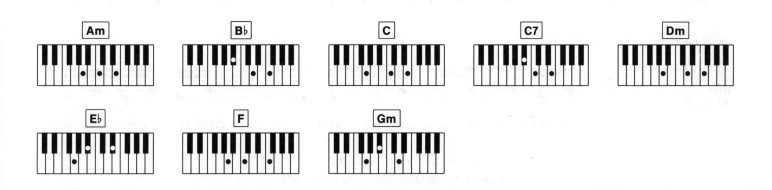

Get Here

Words & Music by Brenda Russell

Suggested Registration: Piano
Rhythm: Ballad
Tempo: ♩ = 54

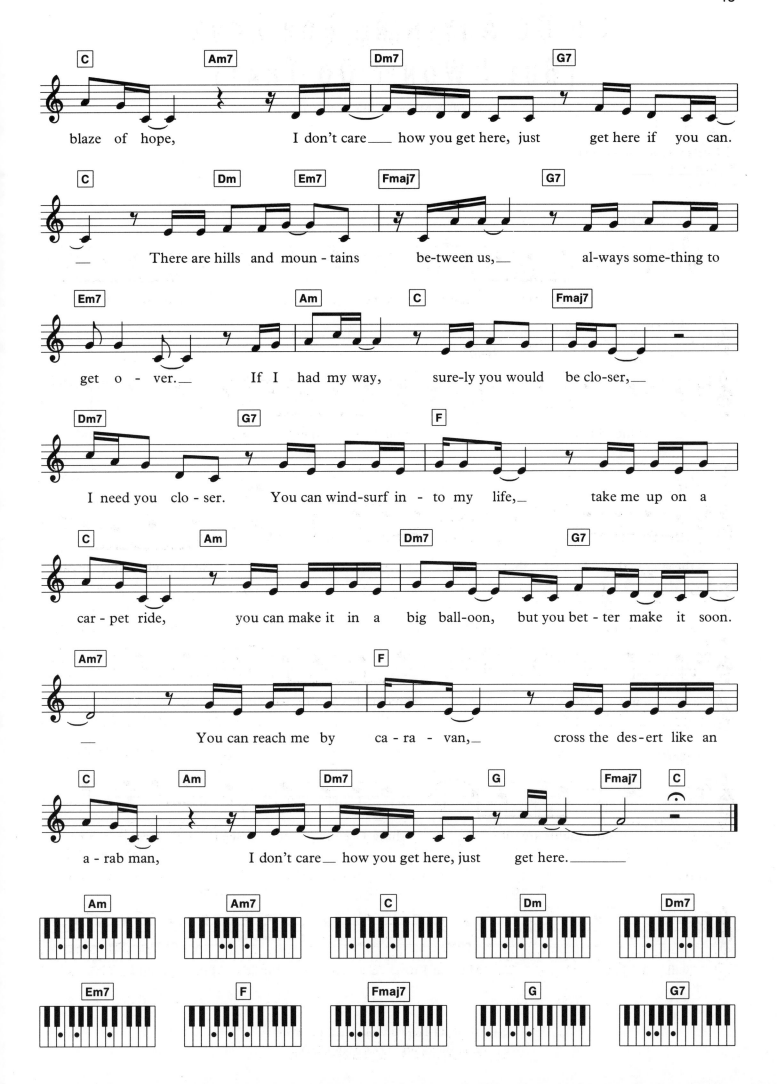

C Am7 Dm7 G7
blaze of hope, I don't care how you get here, just get here if you can.
C Dm Em7 Fmaj7 G7
There are hills and moun - tains be-tween us, al-ways some-thing to
Em7 Am C Fmaj7
get o - ver. If I had my way, sure-ly you would be clo-ser,
Dm7 G7 F
I need you clo - ser. You can wind-surf in - to my life, take me up on a
C Am Dm7 G7
car - pet ride, you can make it in a big ball-oon, but you bet - ter make it soon.
Am7 F
You can reach me by ca - ra - van, cross the des-ert like an
C Am Dm7 G Fmaj7 C
a - rab man, I don't care how you get here, just get here.

Am
Am7
C
Dm
Dm7
Em7
F
Fmaj7
G
G7

I'd Do Anything For Love
(But I Won't Do That)

Words & Music by Jim Steinman

Suggested Registration: Rock Guitar
Rhythm: Rock
Tempo: ♩ = 116

Some days it don't__ come ea-sy, some days it don't __ come hard, some days it don't come__ at all, and these are the days_ that ne-ver end._ Some nights your breath - - ing fire, some nights you're carved__ in ice, some nights are like no - thing I've ev - er seen be - fore,_ or will a - gain. May-be I'm cra - zy, but it's cra - zy, and_ it's_

If

Words & Music by David Gates

Suggested Registration: Acoustic Guitar
Rhythm: Rock Ballad
Tempo: ♩ = 82

I Just Called To Say I Love You

Words & Music by Stevie Wonder

Suggested Registration: Vibraphone
Rhythm: Pop
Tempo: ♩ = 112

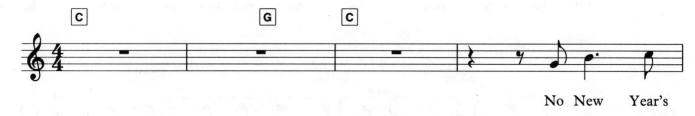

No New Year's

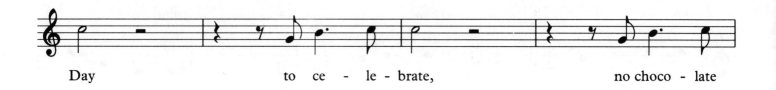

Day   to ce - le - brate,   no choco - late

co - vered can - dy hearts_ to give_ a - way,___   no first of Spring,

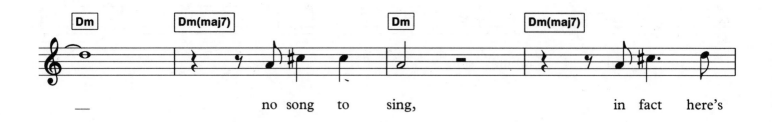

_   no song to sing,   in fact here's

just an - oth - er or - di - na - ry day.___   I just called

to say ____ I love___ you,____ I just called

__ to say____ how much I care,___ I just called

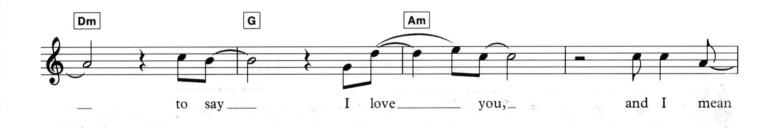

__ to say ____ I love_____ you,_ and I mean

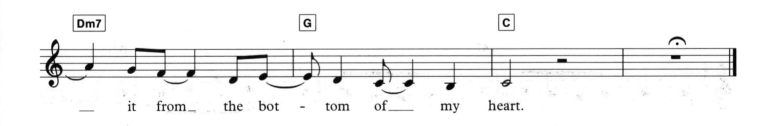

__ it from__ the bot - tom of ___ my heart.

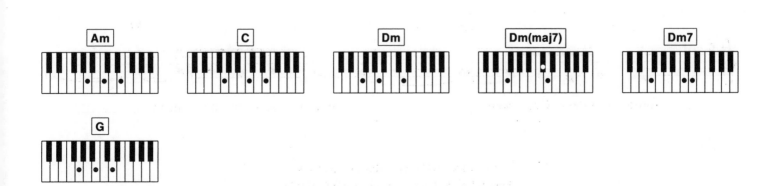

It Had To Be You

Words by Gus Kahn / Music by Isham Jones

Suggested Registration: Jazz Guitar
Rhythm: Medium Swing
Tempo: ♩ = 120

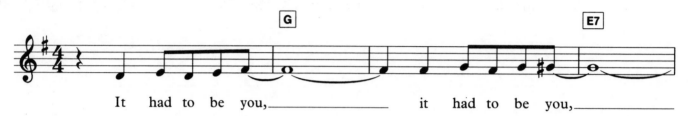

It had to be you,_____ it had to be you,_____

__ I wan-dered a - round,_ and fi - nal - ly found_ the some-bo-dy who_____

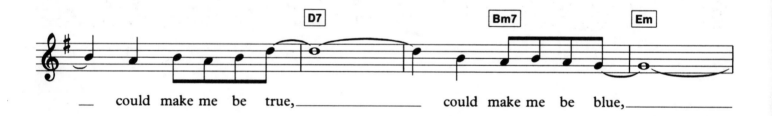

__ could make me be true,_____ could make me be blue,_____

__ and e - ven be glad___ just to be sad,___ think-ing of you._____

__ Some oth - ers I've seen,_____ might ne - ver be mean,_____

© 1924 & 1994 Remick Music Corp., USA

Francis Day & Hunter Ltd., London WC2H 0EA

_ might ne - ver be cross,___ or try to be boss,___ but they would-n't do,_

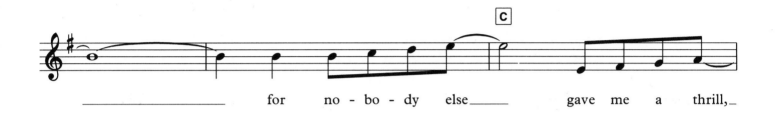

_____ for no - bo - dy else_____ gave me a thrill,_

_ with all your faults___ I love you still.____ It had to be you,_

_ won-der-ful you,___ had to be you._____

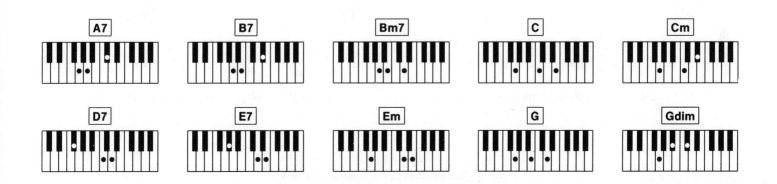

Love Is Here To Stay

Music and Lyrics by George Gershwin and Ira Gershwin

Suggested Registration: Vibraphone
Rhythm: Swing
Tempo: ♩ = 96

It's ve - ry clear

our love is here to stay. Not for a year

but ev - er and a day. The ra - di - o and the

te - le-phone and the mo - vies that we know may just be pass - ing fan - cies

and in time may go. But oh, my dear

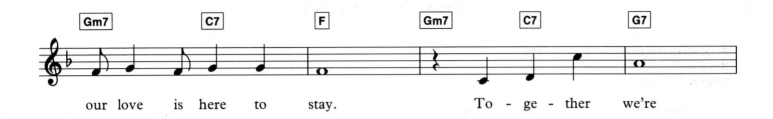

our love is here to stay. To - ge - ther we're

go-ing a long, long way. In time the Rock-ies may crum-ble, Gib -

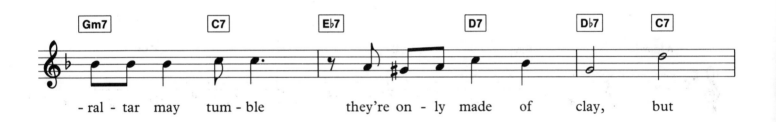

-ral - tar may tum - ble they're on - ly made of clay, but

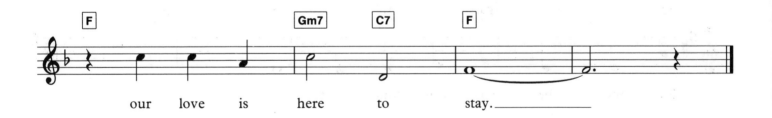

our love is here to stay._____

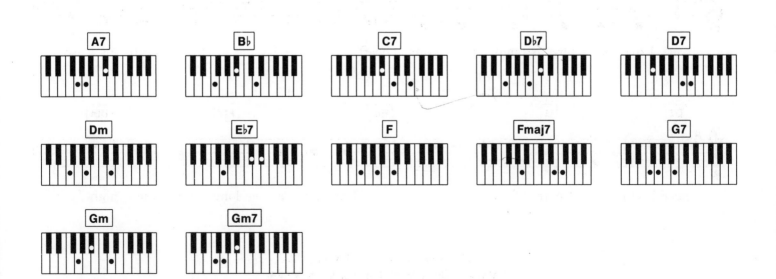

LOVE LETTERS

Words by Edward Heyman / Music by Victor Young

Suggested Registration: Vibraphone
Rhythm: Swing
Tempo: ♩ = 104

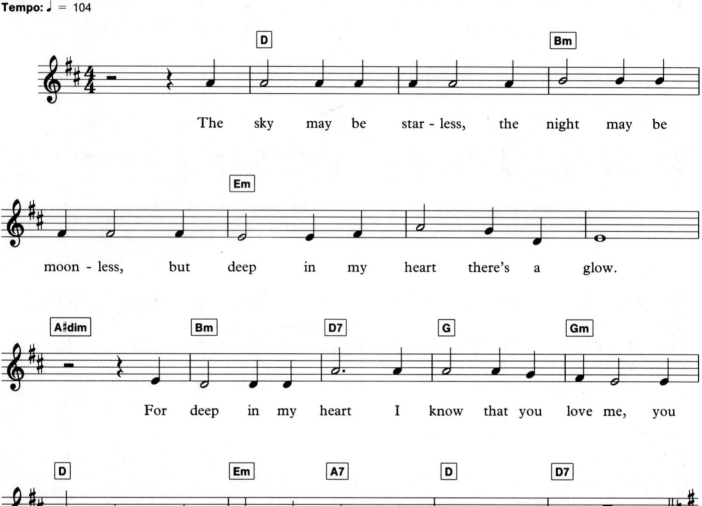

The sky may be star - less, the night may be moon - less, but deep in my heart there's a glow.

For deep in my heart I know that you love me, you love me be - cause you told me so.

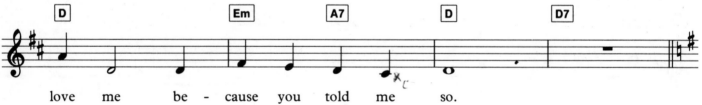

Love let - ters straight from your heart, keep us so

near while a - part. I'm not a - lone in the night,

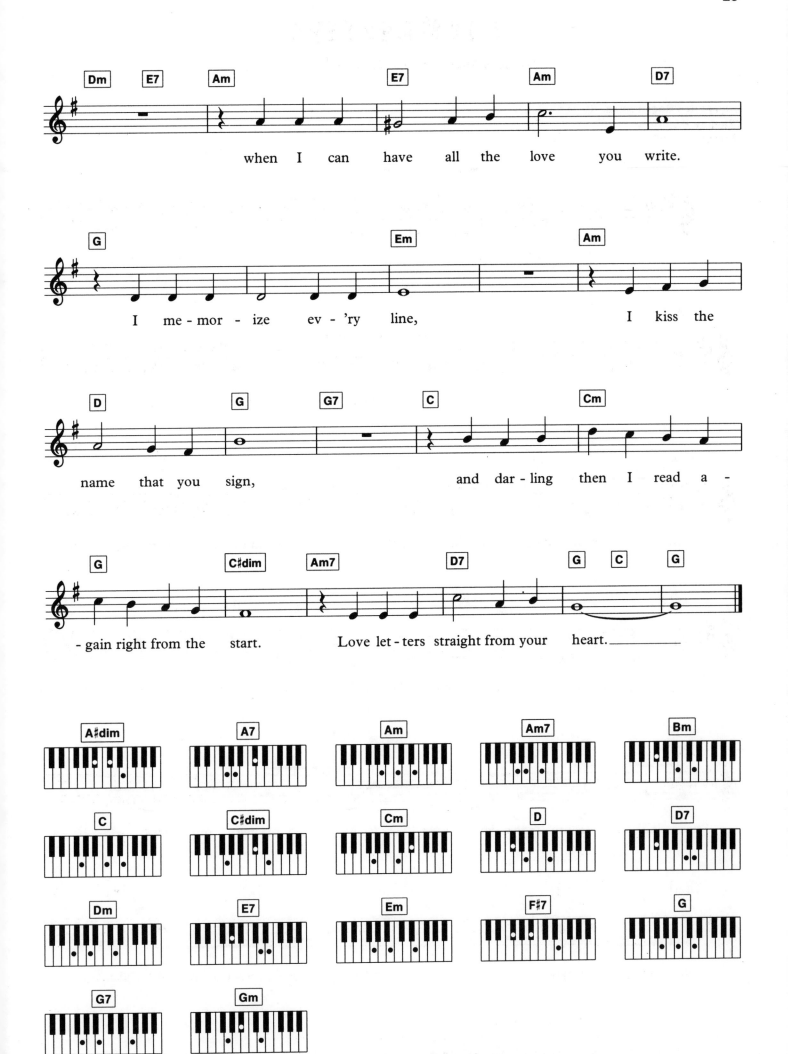

Mandy

Words & Music by Richard Kerr and Scott English

Suggested Registration: Acoustic Guitar
Rhythm: Soft Rock
Tempo: ♩ = 90

I re-mem-ber all my life,____

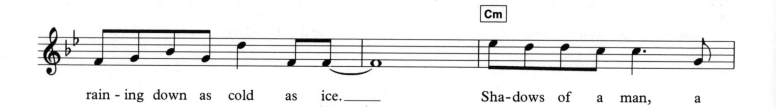

rain-ing down as cold as ice.____ Sha-dows of a man, a

face through a win-dow, cry-ing in the night, the night goes in-to

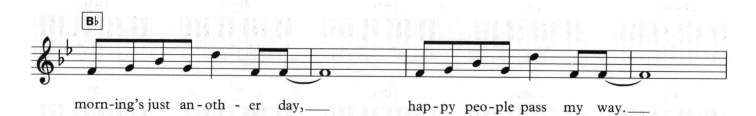

morn-ing's just an-oth-er day,____ hap-py peo-ple pass my way.__

Look-ing in their eyes I see a mem-ory, I ne-ver re-al-ized how

F7 Bb Gm Eb
hap-py you made me. Oh Man - dy, well you came,_ and you gave_ with-out tak -
F F7 Bb
- ing, but I sent you a - way._ Oh Man - dy, well you kissed
Gm Eb F F7
_ me and stopped me from shak - ing,_ and I need you to - day._ Oh
Bb Gm Eb F
Man - dy, well you came,_ and you gave_ with-out tak - ing, but I
F7 Bb Gm Eb
sent you a - way._ Oh Man - dy, well you kissed_ me, and stopped me from shak -
F F7 Gm Eb Bb
- ing,_ and I need you to - day,_ oh Man - dy.

Ab
Bb
Cm
Eb
F
F7
Gm

My Funny Valentine

Words by Lorenz Hart / Music by Richard Rodgers

Suggested Registration: Vibraphone
Rhythm: Slow Swing
Tempo: ♩ = 78-84

My fun - ny Val - en-tine, sweet, co - mic Va - len-tine.

You make me smile with my heart._____

Your looks are laugh - a - ble, un - pho - to - graph - a - ble.

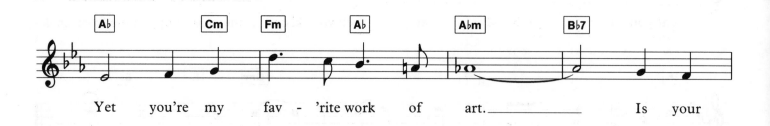

Yet you're my fav - 'rite work of art._____ Is your

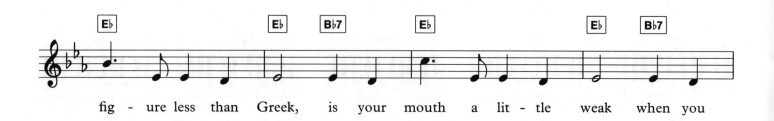

fig - ure less than Greek, is your mouth a lit - tle weak when you

op - en it to speak. Are you smart?_____ But

don't change a hair for me, not if you care for me.

Stay lit - tle Val - en - tine, stay._____

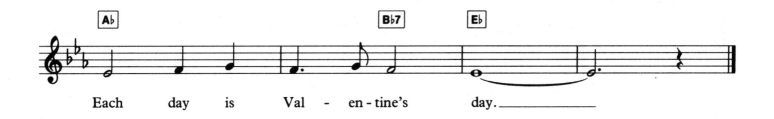

Each day is Val - en - tine's day._____

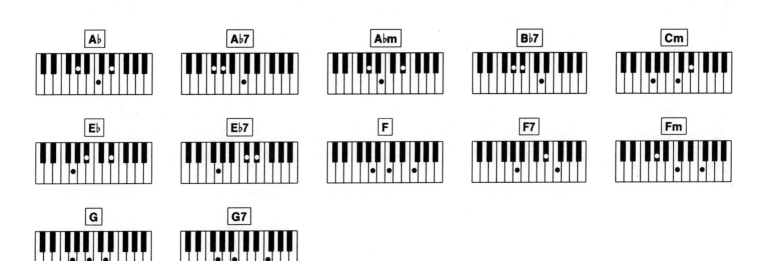

A Nightingale Sang In Berkeley Square

Words by Eric Maschwitz / Music by Manning Sherwin

14 (96)

Suggested Registration: Vibraphone
Rhythm: Slow Swing
Tempo: ♩ = 72

That cer-tain night, the night we met, there was ma-gic a-broad in the

air. There were an - gels din - ing at the Ritz and a night-in-gale sang in

Berke - ley Square. I may be right, I may be wrong, but I'm

per-fect-ly will-ing to swear, that when you turned and smiled at me, a

night-in-gale sang in Berke - ley Square.

The moon that lin-gered o - ver Lon - don town, poor puz - zled moon he

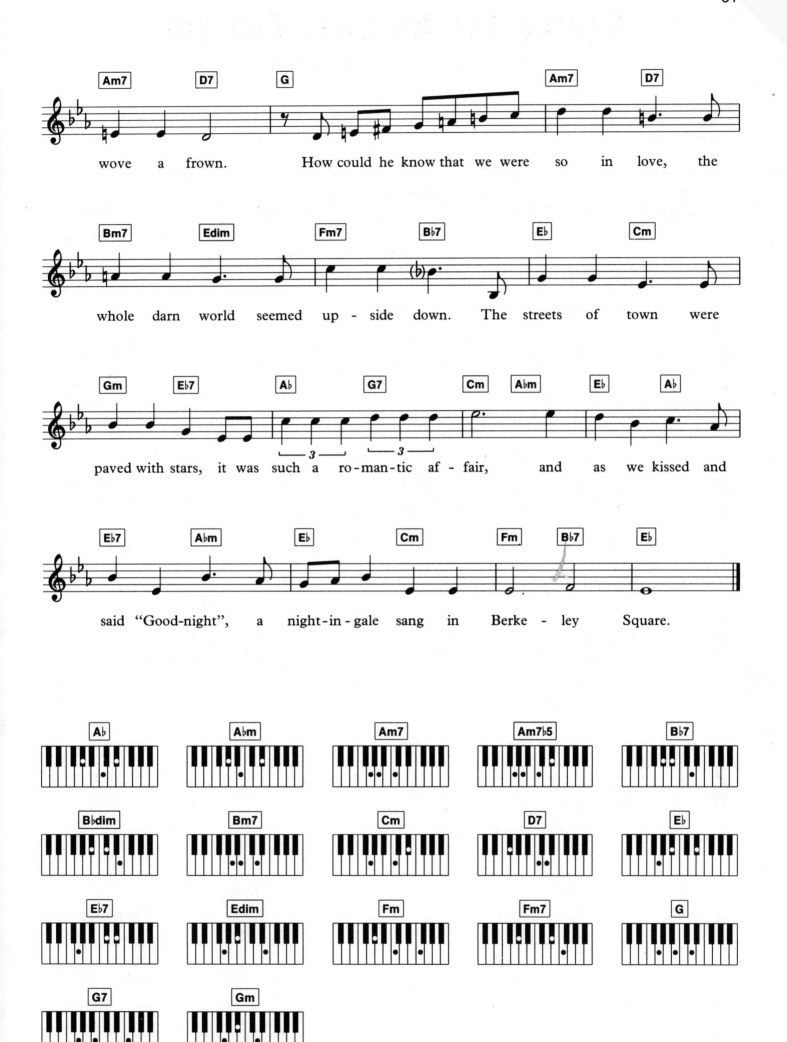

SAVING ALL MY LOVE FOR YOU

Words by Gerry Goffin / Music by Michael Masser

Suggested Registration: Vibraphone
Rhythm: Slow Rock (6/8)
Tempo: ♩. = 64

A few ___ sto - len mo - ments ___ is all ___ that we

share. You've ___ got your fam - 'ly ___ and they ___ need you

there. ___ Though I try ___ to re - sist ___ be - ing last ___ on your

list, but no oth - er man's ___ gon - na do, ___

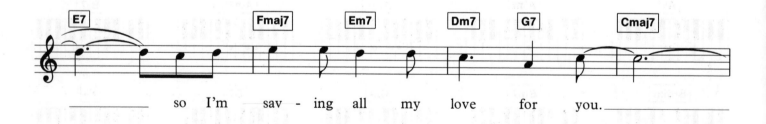

___ so I'm sav - ing all my love for you. ___

___ I've got ___ to get

September Song

Words by Maxwell Anderson / Music by Kurt Weill

Suggested Registration: Jazz Guitar
Rhythm: Swing
Tempo: ♩ = 94

Oh, it's a long, long while from May to De-

-cem - ber, but the days grow short,

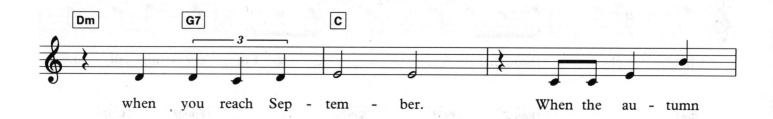

when you reach Sep - tem - ber. When the au - tumn

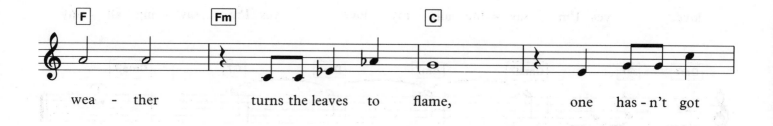

wea - ther turns the leaves to flame, one has - n't got

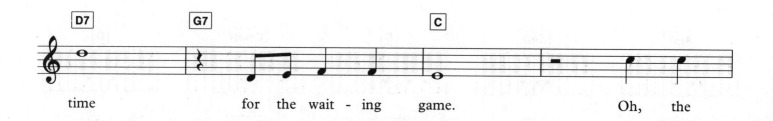

time for the wait - ing game. Oh, the

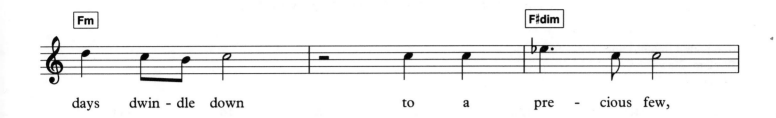

days dwin - dle down to a pre - cious few,

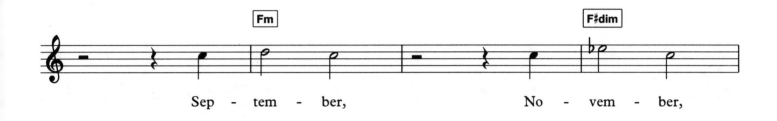

Sep - tem - ber, No - vem - ber,

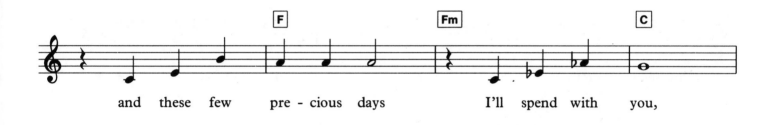

and these few pre - cious days I'll spend with you,

these pre - cious days I'll spend with you._____

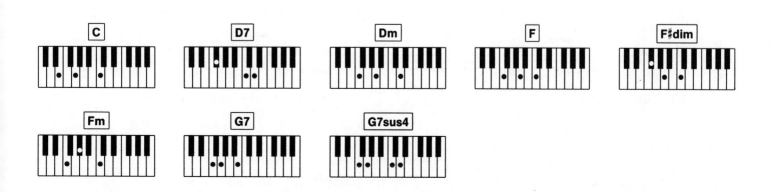

Show Me Heaven

Words & Music by Jay Rifin, Eric Rackin and Maria McKee

Suggested Registration: Tenor Sax
Rhythm: Slow Rock
Tempo: ♩ = 72

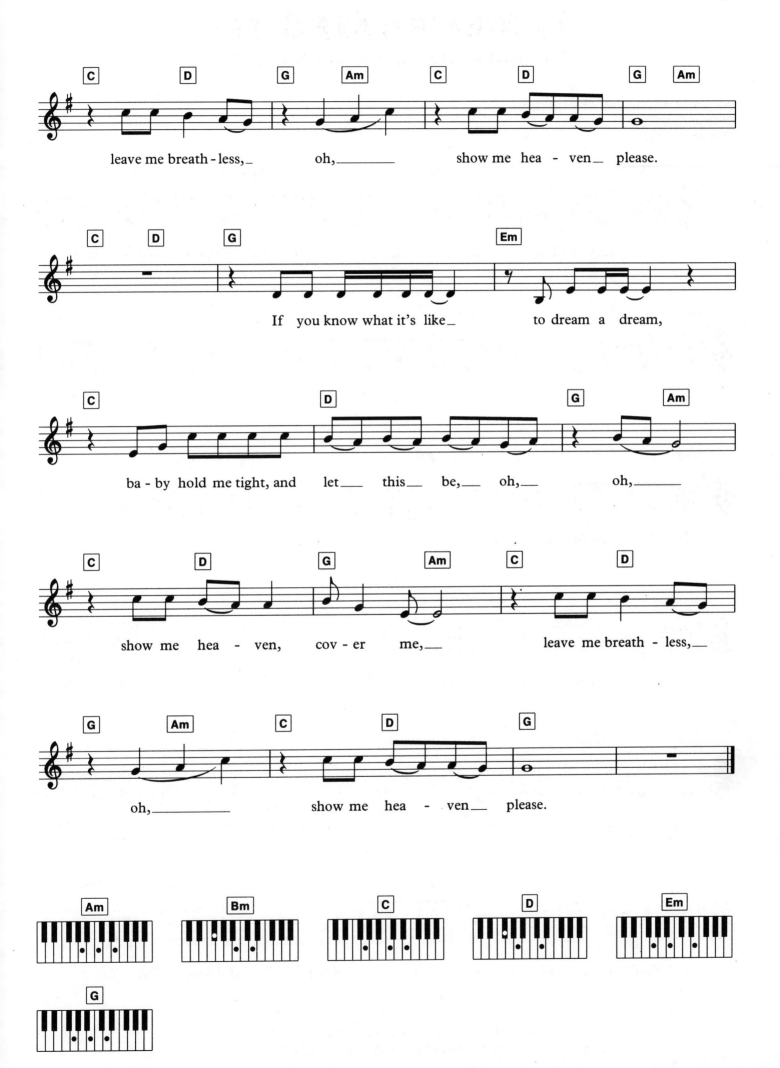

Talkin' In Your Sleep

Words & Music by Roger Cook and Bobby Woods

Suggested Registration: Acoustic Guitar
Rhythm: Soft Rock
Tempo: ♩ = 100

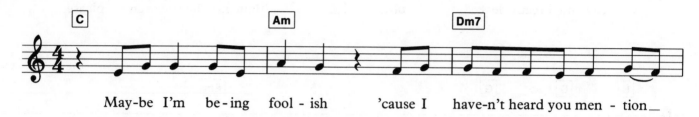

May-be I'm be-ing fool-ish 'cause I have-n't heard you men - tion

a - ny-bo - dy's name_ at all.___ How I

wish I could be sure it's me___ that turns you on

each time you close your eyes. I've

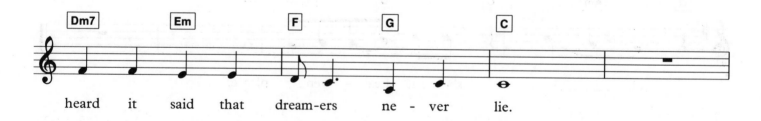

heard it said that dream-ers ne - ver lie.

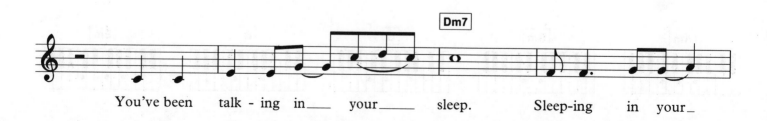

You've been talk - ing in___ your___ sleep. Sleep-ing in your_

Tonight, I Celebrate My Love

Words & Music by Michael Masser and Gerry Goffin

Suggested Registration: Vibraphone
Rhythm: Soft Rock
Tempo: ♩ = 60

TRUE LOVE

Words & Music by Cole Porter

Suggested Registration: Acoustic Guitar
Rhythm: Waltz
Tempo: ♩ = 95

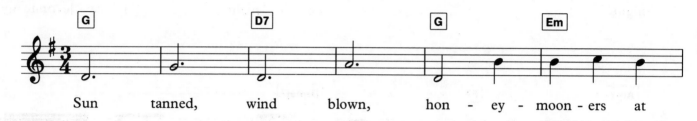

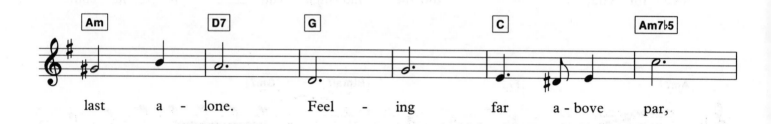

Sun tanned, wind blown, hon - ey - moon - ers at

last a - lone. Feel - ing far a - bove par,

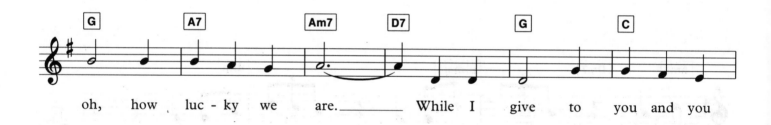

oh, how luc - ky we are._____ While I give to you and you

give to me, true love, true love. So

on and on it will al - ways be, true love,

true love. For you and I have a guard - ian an - gel on

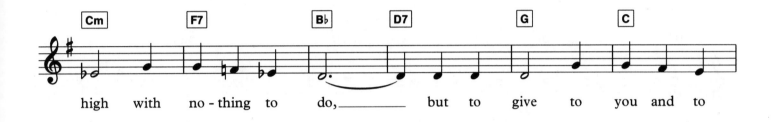

high with no - thing to do,_____ but to give to you and to

give to me love for - ev - er true._____

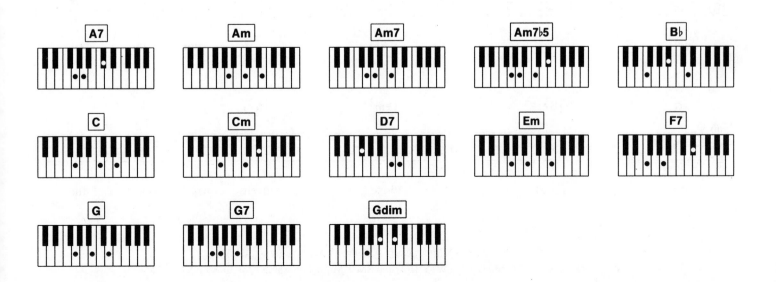

The Twelfth Of Never

Words by Paul Francis Webster / Music by Jerry Livingston

Suggested Registration: Piano
Rhythm: Soft Rock
Tempo: ♩ = 92

WHEN I FALL IN LOVE

Words by Edward Heyman / Music by Victor Young

Suggested Registration: Vibraphone
Rhythm: Slow Swing / Ballad
Tempo: ♩ = 82

When I fall in love, it will be for - ev - er,

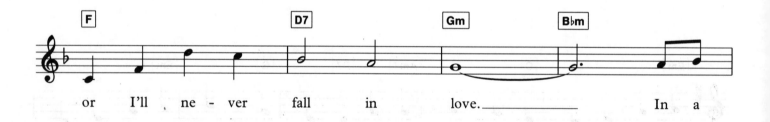

or I'll ne - ver fall in love._____ In a

rest - less world like this is love is end - ed be - fore it's be - gun, and too

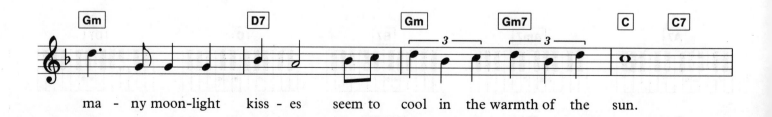

ma - ny moon-light kiss - es seem to cool in the warmth of the sun.

When I give my heart, it will be com - plete - ly,

or I'll ne - ver give my heart._____ And the

mo - ment I can feel that you feel that way too, is

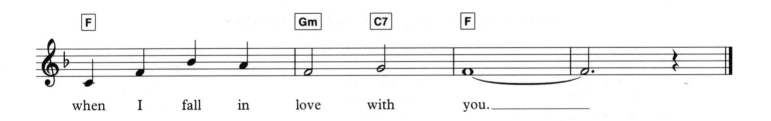

when I fall in love with you._____

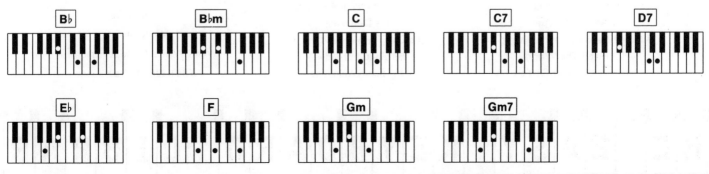

Printed by Watkiss Studios Limited, Biggleswade, Beds. 9/94

THE EASY KEYBOARD LIBRARY
Also Available In this Series

COUNTRY SONGS FOR KEYBOARD

Always On My Mind	Jealousy	Rhinestone Cowboy
By The Time I Get To Phoenix	Jolene	The Rose
Cry	Just When I Needed You Most	Stand By Your Man
Don't It Make My Brown Eyes Blue	Lady	Tie A Yellow Ribbon
Help Me Make It Through The Night	Leaving On A Jet Plane	'Round The Ole Oak Tree
Honky Tonk Man	Me And Bobby McGee	We've Got Tonight
I'm Gonna Sit Right Down And Write Myself A Letter	Rainy Night In Georgia	The Wind Beneath My Wings
I Never Once Stopped Loving You	Red Sails In The Sunset	You've Got A Friend

BIG BAND HITS FOR KEYBOARD

April In Paris	It Had To Be You	September Song
Avalon	It's Only A Paper Moon	A String Of Pearls
Begin The Beguine	La Vie En Rose	Tea For Two
Come Fly With Me	My Heart Stood Still	Thou Swell
Fly Me To The Moon	Night And Day	Tuxedo Junction
Get Happy	Oh, Lady Be Good!	The Very Thought Of You
Indian Summer	On The Sunny Side Of The Street	What Is This Thing Called Love?
In The Mood	Secret Love	

CLASSIC HITS FOR KEYBOARD – VOLUME 1

All Woman	Got My Mind Set On You	Nothing's Gonna Stop Us Now
Coming Around Again	Hanky Panky	The One
Driven By You	I'd Do Anything For Love (But I Won't Do That)	Pray
End Of The Road		Show Me Heaven
Eternal Flame	Like A Prayer	True Colors
From A Distance	Moving On Up	Venus
Get Here	Nobody Does It Better	You're The One That I Want
Go Away	Nothing Compares 2 U	Zoom

CLASSIC HITS FOR KEYBOARD – VOLUME 2

Arthur's Theme	The Greatest Love Of All	My Baby Just Cares For Me
Be My Baby	A Groovy Kind Of Love	My Girl
Careless Whisper	Heal The World	Save The Best For Last
Don't Go Breaking My Heart	Hotel California	This Is It
Don't Let The Sun Go Down On Me	I Got You Babe	Up Where We Belong
Drive	I Just Called To Say I Love You	We Are Family
Fever	In All The Right Places	What A Wonderful World
For Your Eyes Only	Mandy	

SHOWTUNES FOR KEYBOARD

All Of You	I Got Rhythm	Summer Nights
Anything Goes	I Love Paris	The Sun Has Got His Hat On
Embraceable You	I Remember It Well	Tomorrow
Forty-Second Street	It Might As Well Be Spring	True Love
I Am What I Am	It's De-Lovely	Wand'rin Star
I Could Have Danced All Night	Let's Call The Whole Thing Off	Who Wants To Be A Millionaire
If I Ruled The World	Lullaby Of Broadway	You'll Never Walk Alone
I Get A Kick Out Of You	My Funny Valentine	

THE EASY KEYBOARD LIBRARY